WELL-TEMPERED PRAISE II

Piano Arrangements
by
Mark Hayes

T0078483

I'm really proud to bring you my second volume of **WELL-TEMPERED PRAISE**. I hope it will challenge you and give you a fresh appreciation of the songs I've selected. In order to help you make the most of them musically, I've included a few performance notes.

PRAISE TO THE LORD, THE ALMIGHTY

There are many moods within this arrangement, all of which contribute to its drive and excitement. Play it as closely to ♩ =138   as you can, but don't sacrifice accuracy or control for speed. Watch the articulation of the chords on the first page. There are several points of modulation where you'll need to stretch the measure a bit in order to let the ear settle into the new key. Be sure and bring out the melody in the second verse of the arrangement. Slow down enough on the last verse to give it the grandeur and majesty it needs, but keep up the intensity of the tempo to the last note.

HE GIVETH MORE GRACE/NO ONE EVER CARED FOR ME LIKE JESUS

These songs are two of my favorites. Needless to say, they should be played with the freedom and care expressed in the lyrics. Particularly bring out the melody where the chords are thickly voiced and, since I've used many new harmonizations, let the chords linger a bit at special points. The F9 arpeggio near the end of the first song may be improvised if the notes I've indicated do not fit well under your fingers. Actually I usually put in a few **more** notes than that when I play! At the beginning of "No One Ever Cared," please take time with those chords. It can be a very special moment if you give them their due. Also, take the time to figure out all those accidentals. I was **not** trying for the "most complex chord award," but I think you'll enjoy the changes in harmony once you get to know the notes. Notice that I've used the last phrase of "He Giveth More Grace" in the last three 6/8 bars of the arrangement, so be sure and project the melody.

NEO-CLASSIQUE

This piece has more of a classical flavor, one that is purely intentional. Even though there are very simple lines and textures, make the most of them by shaping the phrases creatively. If the trills seem awkward to play they may be left out. At the end of the second ending, take time to breathe musically, and clear your pedal before starting the second section. Also, since the tenth bar of the second section will necessitate a little **ritard** in order to change hand position, don't rush through that measure. Again, at the end of the minor section, take time to breathe before starting the recapitulation. Notice also that the loudest dynamic marking anywhere in the composition is **forte.**

HIGHER GROUND

This is to be played in a traditional black gospel style. If the rolled chords seem a bit awkward, leave them out. Take a special look at what notes are tied in some of the rhythmic sections. Above all, have fun with this, take some risks, and don't lose the energy by being too careful or too academic.

SING HALLELUJAH

In this arrangement of the popular praise chorus, I've tried to expand on the simple melody and chords and turn it into a challenging classical arrangement. The tempo for the "development" section, which starts after the second verse, should be moderately fast. Play the 16th note passages only as fast as you can play them cleanly and well. Pay attention to the abrupt dynamic changes throughout this section and, above all, give it the drama it deserves at whatever tempo you play it. When the main theme returns in F minor at the end, you may want to broaden the tempo some. Also, keep the speed and excitement up in the last seven bars if you can.

ALFRED BURT CAROL MEDLEY

The Alfred Burt Carols are simply delightful, and I would encourage you to locate copies if you're not familiar with them.* The tempo for the first section should be moderately fast, but you can achieve a lot of the life it needs by melody projection, proper pedaling, and crisp articulation. You might find a suitable tempo for the C major section in 4/4 time first, and then use that for the beginning since both tempos should be compatible even though the meter changes. The next two sections need a lot of time and attention to melody projection and to the thick harmonic accompaniment. Be expressive, and don't rush the beginning of "Some Children See Him." The last section may seem a bit awkward at first in E major, but it will fit under your hands easily with a little practice. It should be played, if possible, at the same tempo as the beginning of the medley, but it may need to be a little slower than the first section for some players.

HOW MAJESTIC IS YOUR NAME

Sandi Patti, a leading contemporary gospel singer, has made this new praise song popular in recent months. My arrangement should have a light, almost dance-like quality to it. It is quite rhythmic in character, and special attention should be paid to the articulation I've indicated.

SILENT NIGHT

Savor the different harmonies I've used by taking time at transition points. Think "long phrases" and be sure to keep the melody prominent in the thick chords.

JESUS, KEEP ME NEAR THE CROSS

This arrangement was born from an improvisation I did at a Good Friday service at my church. I've set this old hymn in a minor mode because I think it reflects the seriousness of the lyrics. Notice that the rolled chords are rolled down in the R.H. and up in the L.H. Don't be in a hurry with this setting. Let the whole mood be one of reflection.

RESURRECTION MEDLEY

This arrangement was originally written with Easter Day in mind, but don't limit it to just that occasion. There are several mood changes within the course of this medley. The first is a very free and reflective mood, so be sure and take time with "Low In the Grave." Once you modulate to Eb, do not rush into that tempo. Let the new key feeling settle a bit by gradually working into a fixed tempo. The tempo of "Christ the Lord Is Risen Today" should be determined by how fast you can cleanly play the 16th note passages which come later. Above all, make this section crisp and exciting. In the "Rise Again" section you might want to pay special attention to the melody versus the accompanying melodic passages which occur in the middle of the bars. Keep the last four bars very clean. Notice the pedaling I've indicated.

*Choral arrangements published by Shawnee Press, Inc., Delaware Water Gap, PA 18327.

Get to know these arrangements and don't be frustrated if you can't sightread them perfectly. The extra amount of work you spend on them will be worth it for both you and your listener. May your playing bring praise and glory to God.

Mark Hayes

PRAISE TO THE LORD, THE ALMIGHTY

Words by
Joachim Neander

Music: *LOBE DEN HERREN*
Stralsund Gesangbuch
Arr. by MARK HAYES

HE GIVETH MORE GRACE/
NO ONE EVER CARED FOR ME LIKE JESUS

Arr. by MARK HAYES

* Words by Annie Johnson Flint; music by Hubert Mitchell

NO ONE EVER CARED FOR ME LIKE JESUS*

*Words and music by C.F. Weigle

NEO-CLASSIQUE

MARK HAYES

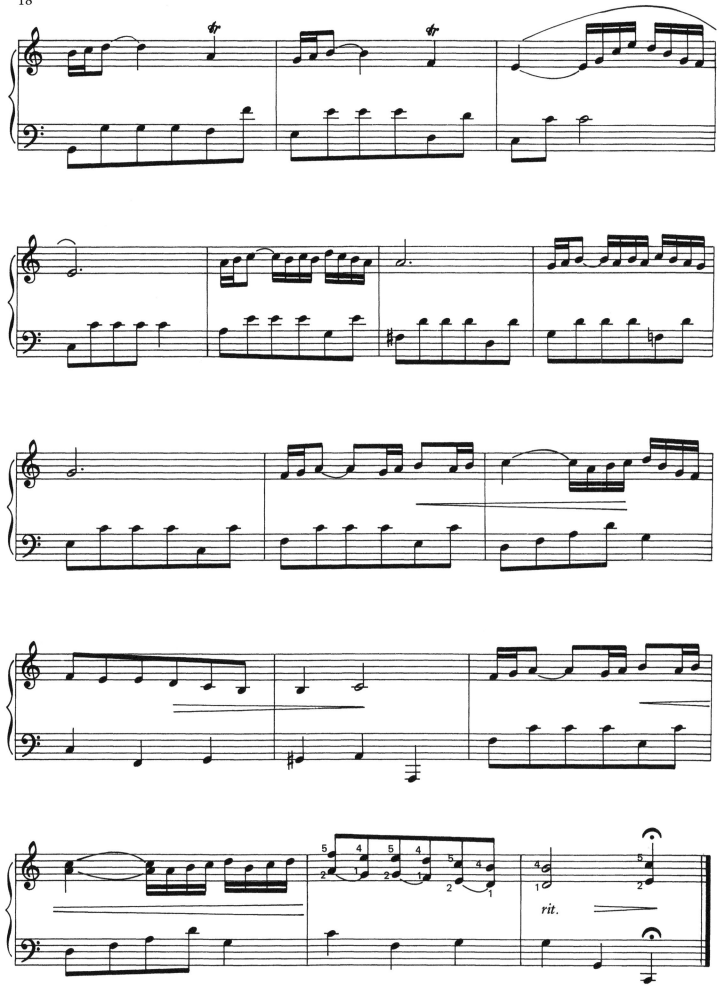

HIGHER GROUND

Words by Johnson Oatman, Jr.

Music by Charles H. Gabriel
Arr. by MARK HAYES

Gospel Rock feel, rhythmically

* To facilitate the playing of the grace note, play the A♯ with the second finger and slide to the B with the same finger.

SING HALLELUJAH

Words and Music by Linda Stassen
Arr. by MARK HAYES

ALFRED BURT CAROL MEDLEY

Words by Wihla Hutson

Music by Alfred Burt
Arr. by MARK HAYES

Moderately fast; lively (♩. = 108)

CAROLING, CAROLING *

bell-like

Warmly ($\dot{\downarrow} \cdot = \dot{\downarrow}$)
a tempo

poco rit.

gva-

(*8va*) - - - - - - - - -   *loco*

* Play octaves if tenths cannot be reached.

THE STAR CAROL *

SOME CHILDREN SEE HIM*

Freely

COME, DEAR CHILDREN *
Lively (♩.=116)

8vb

HOW MAJESTIC IS YOUR NAME

Words and Music by Michael W. Smith
Arr. by MARK HAYES

Lively (♩ = 168)

SILENT NIGHT

Words and Music by Franz Gruber
Arr. by MARK HAYES

JESUS, KEEP ME NEAR THE CROSS

Words by Fanny J. Crosby

Music by William H. Doane
Arr. by MARK HAYES

44

RESURRECTION MEDLEY

LOW, IN THE GRAVE HE LAY!*
Moderately slow; reflectively

Arr. by MARK HAYES

*Words and music by Robert Lowry

Copyright ©1983, GlorySound
A Division of Shawnee Press, Inc.
International Copyright Secured   All Rights Reserved
SOLE SELLING AGENT: SHAWNEE PRESS, INC., DELAWARE WATER GAP, PA 18327

CHRIST THE LORD IS RIS'N TODAY (Jesus Christ is Ris'n Today)*

* Words by Charles Wesley; Tune: Easter Hymn, *Lyra Davidica*

RISE AGAIN*

Grandly; somewhat slower

8vb